First Facts®

Animal Rulers

KINGS OF THE DESERTS

Lisa J. Amstutz

Raintree is an imprint of Capstone Global Library Limited, a company incorporated in England and Wales having its registered office at 264 Banbury Road, Oxford, OX2 7DY – Registered company number: 6695582

www.raintree.co.uk
myorders@raintree.co.uk

Edited by Adrian Vigliano
Designed by Kayla Rossow
Picture research by Kelly Garvin
Production by Kathy McColley
Originated by Captsone Global Library Limited
Printed and bound in India

ISBN 978 1 4747 4861 2 (hardback)
21 20 19 18 17
10 9 8 7 6 5 4 3 2 1

ISBN 978 1 4747 4867 4 (paperback)
22 21 20 19 18
10 9 8 7 6 5 4 3 2 1

British Library Cataloguing in Publication Data
A full catalogue record for this book is available from the British Library.

Acknowledgements
We would like to thank the following for permission to reproduce photographs: Shutterstock: Chris Watson, 9, Don Mammoser, cover (top left), Eduardo Rivero, 13, gabriel12, 21, Galyna Andrushko, cover (middle), gkuna, cover (bottom), gualtiero boffo, cover (top right), 15, John Carnemolla, 11, Laborant, cover (top middle), llyshev Dmitry, 5, Martinez de la Varga, 7, PhumjaiFcNightsky, 19, Richard Seeley, 17; Shutterstock: Alexxxey, Algonga, Gallinago_media, gkuna, Goran J, JeniFoto, Koshevnyk, Ksanawo, mr.Timmi, Pavel K, Perfect Lazybones, rachisan alexandra

We would like to thank Jackie Gai for her invaluable help in the preparation of this book.

Contents

Life in the desert 4

Camel 6

Perentie .8

Dingo 10

Patagonian grey fox 12

Hyena 14

Great horned owl 16

Scorpion 18

Coyote .20

Glossary 22

Find out more 23

Comprehension questions 24

Index 24

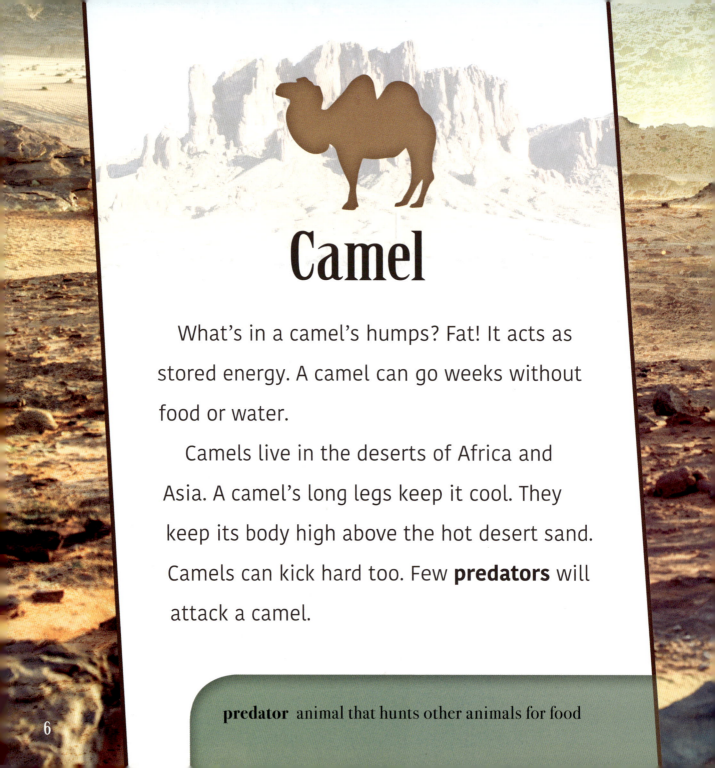

Camel

What's in a camel's humps? Fat! It acts as stored energy. A camel can go weeks without food or water.

Camels live in the deserts of Africa and Asia. A camel's long legs keep it cool. They keep its body high above the hot desert sand. Camels can kick hard too. Few **predators** will attack a camel.

predator animal that hunts other animals for food

Fact! A camel's strong lips can handle eating tough desert plants – even thorny ones!

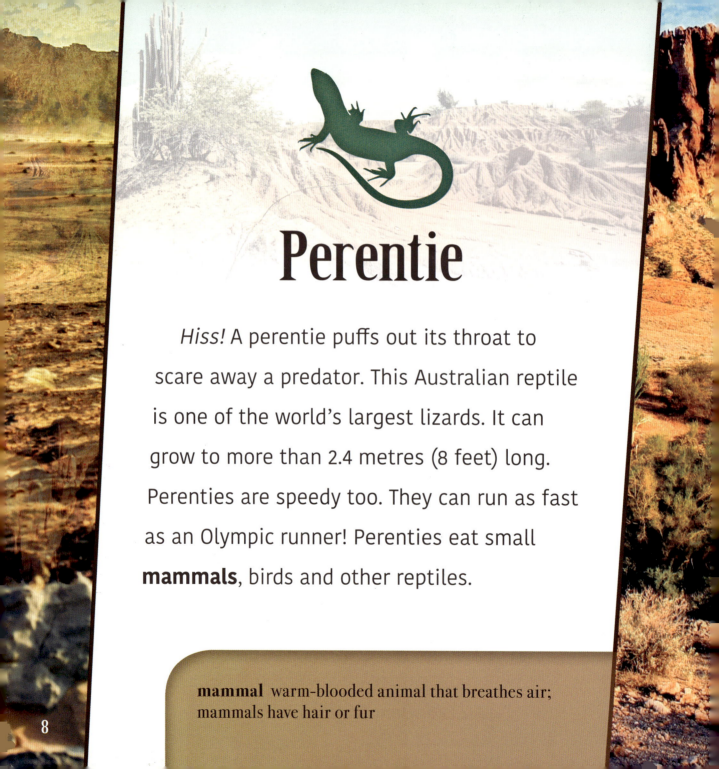

Perentie

Hiss! A perentie puffs out its throat to scare away a predator. This Australian reptile is one of the world's largest lizards. It can grow to more than 2.4 metres (8 feet) long. Perenties are speedy too. They can run as fast as an Olympic runner! Perenties eat small **mammals**, birds and other reptiles.

mammal warm-blooded animal that breathes air; mammals have hair or fur

Dingo

Ah-ooooo! Out in the desert, a dingo howls. Dingoes are the largest meat-eating mammals in Australia. They are similar to both dogs and wolves. Some hunt in **packs**. Dingoes mostly hunt rabbits and wallabies.

pack small group of animals that hunts together

Patagonian grey fox

A Patagonian grey fox twitches its big ears.
It hears a mouse moving under the sand.
Pounce! These South American foxes eat
small animals, fruit, insects and nuts.
They also feed on **carrion**. These foxes are
known for helping one another by bringing
food to other fox families.

carrion rotting flesh of dead animals

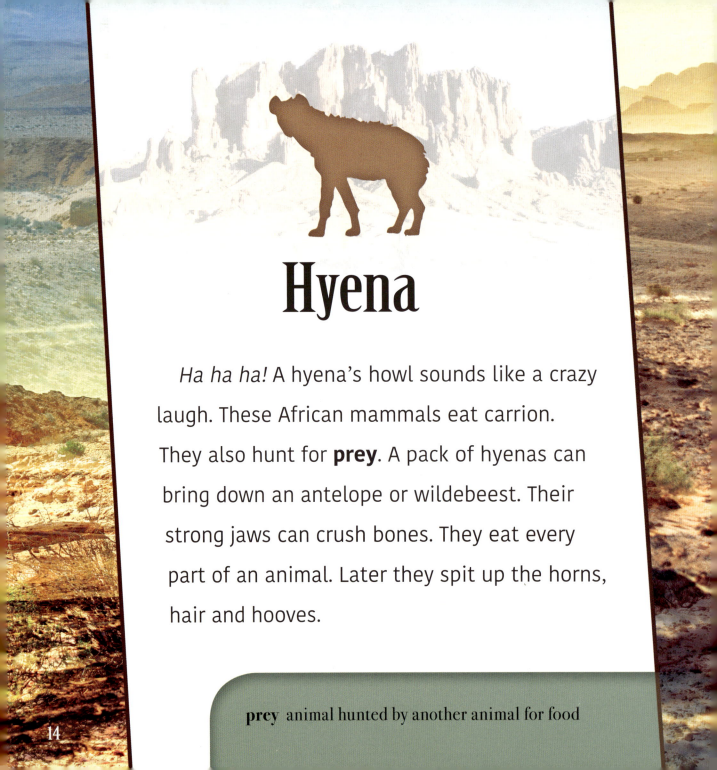

Hyena

Ha ha ha! A hyena's howl sounds like a crazy laugh. These African mammals eat carrion. They also hunt for **prey**. A pack of hyenas can bring down an antelope or wildebeest. Their strong jaws can crush bones. They eat every part of an animal. Later they spit up the horns, hair and hooves.

prey animal hunted by another animal for food

Fact! A hyena's front legs are longer than its back legs.

Great horned owl

Whoosh. In one swoop, a great horned owl snatches a mouse. Then it returns to its cactus perch. Great horned owls live in deserts in North, Central and South America. Their large eyes see well in the dark. Their soft feathers let them fly without making a sound.

Fact! Owls can turn their heads almost all the way around. They can also turn their heads almost upside down!

Scorpion

Look out! A scorpion's stinger carries **venom** for killing prey. Some scorpions are deadly to humans too. Scorpions hunt at night. They eat insects, small mammals and lizards. Their tough **armour** protects them from sun and sand. It also keeps them from drying out. Scorpions live all over the world.

venom poisonous liquid made by an animal to kill its prey
armour bones, scales and skin that some animals have on their bodies for protection

Fact! Some scorpions can slow down their body processes when food is scarce. They can survive on as little as one insect per year!

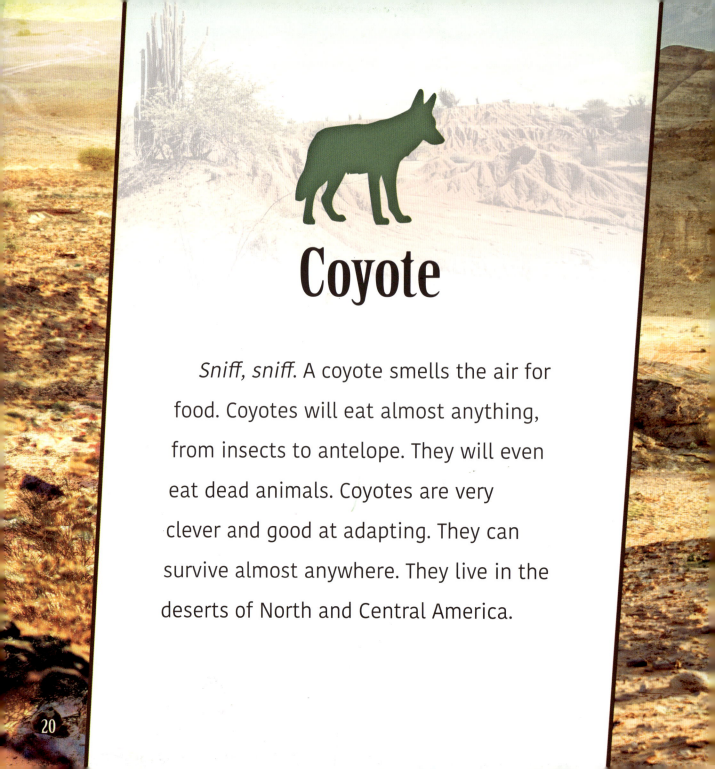

Coyote

Sniff, sniff. A coyote smells the air for food. Coyotes will eat almost anything, from insects to antelope. They will even eat dead animals. Coyotes are very clever and good at adapting. They can survive almost anywhere. They live in the deserts of North and Central America.

Fact! Coyotes sometimes hunt together in packs.

Glossary

adapt change to fit into a new or different environment

armour bones, scales and skin that some animals have on their bodies for protection

carrion rotting flesh of dead animals

environment air, water, trees and other parts of the natural world

mammal warm-blooded animal that breathes air; mammals have hair or fur

pack small group of animals that hunts together

predator animal that hunts other animals for food

prey animal hunted by another animal for food

venom poisonous liquid made by an animal to kill its prey

Find out more

Books

Camels (Meet Desert Animals), Rose Davin (Raintree, 2017)

Desert Food Chains (Food Chains and Webs), Angela Royston (Heinemann Library, 2014)

Deserts (What Animals Live Here?), M J Knight (Franklin Watts, 2016)

Websites

www.bbc.co.uk/guides/zsqnfg8
This BBC website has information about what a desert is and which animals live in the desert.

www.dkfindout.com/uk/earth/deserts/what-is-desert
Find out more about deserts on this website.

Comprehension questions

1. Name three animals that dingoes prey on.

2. How does a scorpion's body help it survive in the desert?

3. How do a Patagonian grey fox's ears help it hunt?

Index

adaptations 4, 20

feathers 16
fruit 12

humans 18
hunting 10, 14, 18, 21

insects 12, 18, 19, 20

mice 12, 16

rabbits 10

stingers 18

wallabies 10